Gallery Books
Editor: Peter Fallon
CLIMBING THE LIGHT

Pearse Hutchinson

CLIMBING THE LIGHT

Gallery Books

Climbing the Light
is first published
on 20 November 1985
in paperback and in a
clothbound edition
by The Gallery Press.

The Gallery Press
19 Oakdown Road
Dublin 14. Ireland.

© Pearse Hutchinson 1985

All rights reserved

ISBN 0 904011 86 0 (*paperback*)
 0 904011 87 9 (*clothbound*)

Grateful acknowledgement is made to the editors of *The Cork Examiner*, *Cyphers*, *The First Ten Years: Dublin Arts Festival Poetry*, the *Galway Civil Rights Broadsheet* and *Poetry and Audience* in which some of these poems have appeared.
The Gallery Press receives financial assistance from The Arts Council / An Chomhairle Ealaíon, Ireland.

Contents

The Cap *page* 9
Brown with No Whites 10
She Made her False Name Real 12
The Flames are False: Only the Hell is Real 14
The Kid on the Mountain 15
Amhrán na mBréag 18
Driscoll 5: Glories Clear 19
Flames 21
Miracles 22
Findrum 23
To Maria Spiridonovna on her Keeping 24
After Breaking My Own Foot in France 26
Dream 27
The Goat 28
Plums 29
Leper-slit 30
Orgy 32
The Poet Rides on Horseback through the Night 33
Affection 36
Burnham Deepdale 37
Clear the Stove in the Morning 39
Flowering Stump 41
Bright Red Berries 43
Bad Milk 44
A True Story Ending in False Hope 45
Traffic-lights are Dangerous 47
Manifest Destiny 49
Climbing High 51
The Lost Garden 52
Elexía do Caurel 53
Andalusia 54
A Colour-Photo 55
Notes 56

To Justin O'Mahony
(1943-79)

The Cap

The cap I wanted to wear tonight I couldn't lay hands on:
light-brown crumpled corduroy
forgotten overnight in a flat I was two years transient in
by a Ballyconnell truck-driver. When Francis came round
   the next morning
he said 'It's raining, you lost your best beret last week and can't
   find one in the whole of Leeds:
keep the cap. Peter makes good money, loses a cap a month,
   buys a new cap every month'.
Peter I'd never try to imitate
the way you put the hint of a liquid y
between the c and the a in that word cap.
But Peter it kept my head warm and dry
for two long years and more. I brought it across on the plane,
had to cram it on because of the driving tarmac rain,
it made a couple of customs-officers look crooked at me.
I had my hands deep
in the pockets of a plastic mac
and that was sopping too,
but Peter the main road to Cavan gets kinder every ell,
warmer every magpie, every barefoot blackbird.

Brown with No Whites

for Michael Augustin

A young brown pony in a green Gloucester field
trotting gently up to a mottled wall
dandling its big head across looking for company.

Giant brown eyes, unanswerable, softly questing,
no whites.
                A timid human hand was not repulsed.

From our side a dove-grey pregnant cat
climbed in a stately fashion across the wall
to bask in sunlight on a stone slab
                                near the pony,

Who warily bent the sturdy neck down
to nuzzle the microscopic furry creature —
fellow, perhaps, creature —
and friends were made. She rolled around on the warm grey stone,
the pony moved her about with his nose, they played tip-and-tig and
    conkers, they played like lovers
who never guessed that love could be anything but fun.
The pony and the cat making friends made a human being happy.

But then someone told him, in friendly jest,
the name of the pony was
Leprechaun.
                (As who might say Shillelagh, Rastus, Brit.)
Green English fields turned orange —
like a decoration on a Cabinet-Minister's breast;
the wall grew higher between the pony and me.

But no pony deserves a name so tawdry;
so the same human hand, less timid now,
reached out again and, even less repulsed,
re-named this animal — what's in a pony's name? —
a name less flippant, a friend's name,
a tree's name.
Other trees bore witness to that rechristening:
apple, sycamore, holly.
Gloucester fields turned green again,
the sky as blue again
                    as ever over Wormwood Scrubs.
'Macdara', said the man to the pony,
'play with your heavy grey cat. A mhac', ar sé,
'ná bí ag briseadh cait: brisfear luath go leor í.'
Wishing human beings had never called each other names
less than human, less than ponies, less than cats.
The cat went on playing with the pony,
like plover basking in a meadow full of sheep.

She Made her False Name Real

When the Holy Office descended upon us to make us all saints,
to change our names with tongues of flame,
to make us all saints instead of the devils they
knew
    we
        were
            under pain of all those tongues,
of turning not living devils but most unholy ghosts,
we changed our names, not being martyrs, to the names
    they gave us.

A change of name's a trivial thing:
it only leads to centuries of bitterness.

Nahara ben Abrafim became
                      Arnau Albertí
and remained a good Catholic for ever.
Isach Leví became
                Bernat Aguiló.
Mahabuf Faquim became
                    Joan Amat —
he was John the Beloved for ever.
Magaluf ben Salem became
                    Pere Cases.

What Marc Despont was called before the change
nobody knows:
                his Jewish name is not recorded.
What Joan Martí was called before the change
is not recorded:
                perhaps a descendant of his,
changing only one vowel,
                gave his life for the freedom of Cuba.

Jacob Prehensal became
Andreu Rossinyol: Andrew the Nightingale.
Felip Umbert had been
               Isach ben Magaluf.

When every convert on the island sported
   a brand-new holy name,
the priests came round to smoke out Yiddish vestiges.
We all hastened to bless ourselves and bless ourselves and bless
   ourselves, not being martyrs,
only carpenters and tailors and bookbinders
and the best cartographers in Europe,
yes we all blessed ourselves like crazy
except an old woman called Jaumeta
whose surname is not recorded
nor even her first name before the change.
But she was imprisoned for eight days on bread-and-water —
mild enough for our enlightened times —
and that old woman made her name real,
she made the name the Christians forced upon her
Jewish and real and Christian beyond their burning.

The Flames are False: Only the Hell is Real

for Carmelo Sánchez

My name was Gaietà Ripoll, if I had lived
in your enlightened times I'd have had to sign
myself not Gaietà
but Cayetano, like,
as in this limbo some drowned men enlighten me,
Dudley for Darach.

Not only my name they distorted:
progress distorted their vengeance:
for I had the privilege of being the last
culprit the Holy Office killed.
They should have burnt me,
but they only hanged me:
the Church, like mankind, was making headway.
Shamefaced, they were *shame*-faced.
But nostalgic.

So shame and nostalgia, as creative a mésalliance
as Christ and the moneychangers, painted a cardboard expanse
with flames, the flames of hell, the glory-holes of their own minds,
the purgatories of their misnomers;
that cardboard hellfire held beneath my gallows,
until my dancing stopped.
I danced above their cardboard flames.
Their compromise between shame and bloodlust
drizzled
        above the phoney flames of bad faith.
My name was Gaietà Ripoll. My last words were:
Crec en Déu.

The Kid on the Mountain

for Vincent Woods

What colours can we call them,
the earth and stone that took our eyes in youth,
and now come back with all the pain and beauty
of lost youth itself?

Light-brown,
        fawn,
umber, sienna, inaccuracies,
even honey: that old myth.

The colour, the shade,
              changes
from stone to stone in the same building,
from field to foothill.

Warmth
not heat:
warmth built by human hands for the heat to warm,
and for the centuries of eyes, our eyes,
to warm their hands at,
to warm our speaking hearts at.

Warmth by light out of time:
a mane of colour streaming down
the soft hard back of time.

When I was twenty-seven the Málaga foothills
the light-brown colour of a young goat caught
on Kilmashogue when I was eleven then skittering out of our grasp
then caught again, kept; the nap, the burlap eye-feeling,
of clay and kid.

Climbing the light — never say pale, never —
brown foothills on the opposite slope
across the dry river the goats were black

but kept in the mind as a rough, soft, warm fawn
was kept on Kilmashogue for a day, let go,
but kept in the mind until its river dries.

Climbing we heard and saw
cicadas 'a tremble of light in the leaves' of the olive-trees
and rapping the trees' rough skin, hurting knuckles,
we put their tremble out
                      for a long minute but then
they started up again:
they were the sound of heat and the earth was the colour
   of warmth.

Remember at thirty-four (was that still beauty and pain?)
crossing the Pyrenean frontier breaking bread together,
for the first time together in that beloved country,
the good strong Spanish bread that needs no butter —
the countryside a disappointing green:
that wasn't what we came for, that wasn't our need
(but theirs, but theirs!)
the fierce red earth
in the olive-orchards — that was a different nettle,
we grasped it with all our eyes and how it stung us
into life and how we stung it back!

But the calm
        light
               brown
the golden stone

the myth of honey serene on golden churches
the shades
          changing
from brick to brick from Font
Romeu to Sant Climent:
serene stone
answering a sky that's both serene and fierce
the silent stone speaking in colour
one colour answering another
one silence speaking
to the other: Hands
climbing the sky through fashioned earth,
bringing the earth and sky together,
stone breathing time,
a compact church a tall
bell-tower
making a span of earth and sky,
a trinity of earth and craft and sky
as holy and almost as lovely
as any implacable blue.

But I remember better —
though stone outlast us, I can still hear —
a small goatherd singing
in a high, thin, clear voice,
half-Gregorian but more blithe,
on the opposite hill across a dry
riverbed, his black goats meandering.
He'd be in his thirties now, let's hope.
Let's hope.

The riverbeds go dry, the fountains climb,
the warm colours grow.

Amhrán na mBréag

In the middle of the wood I set sail
as the bee and the bat were at anchor just off shore
I found in the sea's rough shallows a nest of bees
In a field's ear I saw
a mackerel milking a cow
I saw a young woman in Greece boiling the city of Cork over the
  kitchen fire
Last night, in a serpent's ear, I slept sound
I saw an eel with a whip in her hand whipping a shark ashore
MacDara's Island told me he never saw more
wonders:
a kitten washing a salmon in the river
the music-mast of a ship being
conceived in a cat's arse
a badger in the nest of an eagle milking a cow
and a sparrow wielding a hammer putting a keel on a boat.

after Micheál Mharcais Ó Conghaile

Driscoll 5: Glories Clear

A woman went to Stephen's Green, taking her three sons, to meet a nine-year-old boy, close friend of her son his age. They waited, as arranged, by the pond in the Green, where the beautiful ducks are fed or stoned. In the Green, where twenty years before Driscoll had seen black be beautiful and blond be beautiful together, seen

> miscegenation make its glories clear.

They waited by the summer pond, to go with that boy, their friend, to Bewley's Oriental Café for a summer treat: cool milkshakes, iced coffee, cakes. They waited for half-an-hour, three-quarters, gave him up, left; and as they came out the Arch, there the boy was waiting, near the mobile X-Ray unit, near help, so they went and had the treat but after a time he came out with it, why he'd not waited inside the Green, by the peaceful water, not kept exactly the appointed place, the beautiful incomparable safety, the irreplaceable warmth, of a definite appointment with friends: 'I didn't want to go in alone', he said, 'they call me "nigger"; when I go in with you' (he turned to her son his age, his friend) 'they're afraid to say it but when I go in alone . . .'

> to Stephen's Green, where
> ignorance makes its miseries clear.

Two days later, brooding on this, Driscoll, grey in the face as always, entered a telephone-kiosk on Stephen's Green, opposite Emmet, who died for freedom, his cool green lissome strength, his vibrant stone challenge, a stone's throw from the College of Surgeons, the Hippocratic oath, help — and the first thing he saw, on the pale-grey inner wall of the kiosk was, in exquisite lettering, in rich bright black: 'Dirty nigger whore'.

The boy is nine, now. An Irish woman gave him birth. It could
be, it was meant to be, his Green.

He's only nine, now. What danger will become? Of him? Of
those mocking schoolchildren? well schooled . . .

This happened in Dublin
    to a child.
This happened in a capital city
    in the '70s.
In sunlight, in summer,
    by water, near trees.
This happened
    among children
            to a child.
The mindless make their glories clear.

Flames

A red setter leaping
constant up and down, up-and-down,
like a big, living flame
in a dark slum room
where an old poor woman lies in bed sick,
the heat cut off the light cut off,
her only light her only heat
the red-gold setter leaping
tireless up and down like a tall
sinuous brilliant almost healing flame.

Never such buoyancy, never!

A long skinnymalink with auburn hair
loose-limbed in his mid-thirties
immaculate in a flame-coloured suit,
leaping up and down, up-and-down,
like a loose-haired flame
in a bar at the head of the Zeedijk
at one in the morning as Justin
played planxties on the penny-whistle.
Such Amsterdancing! He couldn't get enough of it.
Vertical wavering, a grace, a flame.

Never such buoyancy, never!

Miracles

You were my last miracle, as I was your
miracle, though not your last,
no never your last, only one
of many, though for each of us your best.

Your generosity
taught me to counter jealousy, your feast
of gleaming white bread (rich black crust)
worked wonders, filled and blessed
my long emptiness.
I was hungry and you fed me.
I was dying and you raised me from the dead.

Miracles, though we have not been led to
believe it, are always done
by the one in need as well
as the one who harrows
both heaven and hell.

Had you been less lavish
   with your miracles,
I'd still be starving
   in the wilderness.

Though bittern and cormorant nest
in the ruins of your feast,
though the bitter beak tear my breast
that cannot forget
your gleaming, sheltering breast,
we stole fire together
from hell in a fennel-stalk:
you were my last
miracle, and my best.

morning, September 1981

Findrum

Findrum:
the same room:
6 a.m.
10 years later, and I am
still here,
sitting in a similar
though not the same
armchair,
and not gazing
at you naked
asleep on the bed
nor waiting
but only staring
at an empty, sagging bed.

Oh for you to be here
and we could sag it more:
even break it
right down to the floor!

To Maria Spiridonovna on her Keeping

To Maria Spiridonovna on her keeping
in the hungry Moscow of 1920
a friend brought
        eggs and cherries.
I'd love to know what colour they were:
white eggs and black cherries,
brown eggs and red cherries —
or duck-blue?
'Who's for duck-blue cherries?'

Does it matter what colour they were?
It matters everything,
        and not at all.

One of the country-people Maria had spent years in jail for
    under the Czar
smuggled to her in hiding, in gratitude,
when she was nearly starving,
hiding from the betrayers of the revolution,
eggs and cherries to eat.
One of those country-people who'd smuggled letters to her
    from many parts of Russia,
asking her to tell them if this new October Christ
had so soon been crucified again,
smuggled to Maria in her need
eggs and cherries to eat.

And Maria smuggled them into the knapsack of her comrade
who was leaving on a dangerous mission
against the dictators who'd betrayed
the revolution, and Maria Spiridonovna, and black cherries,
    and the people.

Then she reached up to his tall arm
and stroked it.

He went on his mission, let's hope the danger gave him time
to find those eggs, those cherries
dripping with love — with 'bourgeois sentimentality':
 so regrettably common
among the rustic proletariat, not yet made over,
among the deprived.
But does it matter? Whether he found them? Or what colour
 they were?
It used to matter before the dreams were broken:
the upstart bourgeois dream of safety —
the ancient human dream of freedom.

15 September 1978: Wexford

After Breaking My Own Foot in France

My little wandering limb the splint must thole:
it brings me nearer my dear one to console.
How poor a friend I'd be, examined home,
if, his bone broken, I broke not my own.

from the Irish of Pádraigín Haicéad

Dream

Cumbersome, the dream said, cumbersome.
What's the Gaelic for cumbersome? Find out,
 the dream commanded.
Somnambulist fingers hefted the huge new dictionary,
flicking the pages to the third letter:
coll, the hazel-tree, as the older lexicon told.
But cumbersome wasn't to be found in the new book,
even by fingers who thought themselves long accustomed.
A phleidhce! said the dream, exasperated,
'amadáin chríochnaithe! you call yourself literate
and you don't know yet that Kumbersome begins with a *K!*
K u m   b e r   und so weiter.

So the fingers dread-fast in the dream scrabbled
in mild guilt for the letter *K*,
though somewhere in the back of their mind they had
 a resentful feeling
the letter *K* unlike the letter *V*
had never grown a Gaelic tree.
But scrabbling brought no news, no Kumbersome,
and suddenly it dawned on the fingers they were hunting
 an English word in an Irish-English dictionary
and it wasn't Ó Dónaill they needed at all but the other,
 darker blue
and somebody'd borrowed that blue and forgotten to give
 it back
so the fingers looked daggers at the dream,
or shrugged, or splayed,
and the dream let them off with a warning.

The Goat

I spoke to a goat.
She was tied up alone in a field.
Fed-up with grass,
rain-soaked, bleating.
That plaint was a brother
of my own suffering, so I
replied, at first for fun
and then because suffering's eternal,
it has one voice, and never alters.
That voice I heard
sobbing in a lonely goat.
In a goat with a Jewish face
I heard all hurt complain,
all other life.

from the Italian of Umberto Saba

Plums

When the dreamer found her she was in the cradle,
in a merendero beside no sea,
the nuns were looking after this orphan,
she was two years old the morning the dreamer found her.

Her little body was a glow of plums:
translucent —
each one translucent:
pale green
plums like pale green grapes;
the shape and the lustre of plums
but the pale green.

It took the dreamer two years to track her down,
he'd been roaming after her ever since he heard of her birth,
and now that he found her she was all fruit,
only a fruit-cluster,
and when he moved his hand to touch her,
she dwindled to a word:
translucent.
The dreamer like the dream
dwindling.

Leper-slit

Aluminium glinting faintly in a shuttered kitchen,
electric lights switched off, the faint sun
stealing in — the antique shutters
don't quite meet —
that's what life can be like: a leper-slit,
what splendor! the eye could glimpse
only part of — the sermon's paunch, not lips,
but listen — could lepers hear? unglazed the slit let
thin billows of incense out (could the leper-king smell,
or choke on peace, who never choked on war,
or choke on talk of peace?)

Are we all kings? All lepers? All both?
One day the leper fitting his yearning to the narrow bright groove,
his azure hands on either side clutching the gargoyle stone,
met another darkling eye: the lonely, bored parson
mad to escape the drafty, crampt chapel
into the wide leprosarium,
the kingly outside world:
the porch, too sanctified, no exit,
the stained glass unbreakable,
sacrilege a man-trap or makeshift —
only the thin leper-window could let him out —
could his billowing soul fit,
like incense, through? Each gaze
recoiled, then the leper let go of the gargoyles,
and rolled around in stitches on the grass;
the parson rolled in the nave; but he was more
of a gargoyle than the leper,
and he'd glimpsed what was left of regal
in the leprous gaze — here
the chronicle breaks off (the stubborn scriptorium
no doubt invaded by even more civilized barbarians,

a tiny golden yearling pocketed, habit hitched up in a scurry),
eras later, bulldozer found
adhering to the sides of the leper-slit
shreds of a soul — soiled silk;
in the nave, crushed elderberries,
and wound around the gargoyle's ear
a charm against the plague.

But lepers have been known to ring
their bells against the belfries,
and when at last I folded back the antique shutters
they creaked, peeled, muffled
for a moment the leaking roof, the sun poured in,
not faint; I put the aluminium on for tea,
the apple-tree was at last in full flower,
and the leper-slit, a fossil theory, divine right,
lay in the grass among bright-yellow weeds,
lower than a snake in a waggon-track, awaiting
its own antarctic truck.

Orgy

'Let's go somewhere else and have an orgy'
you said with a happy smile to the other five of us
holding an Irish kaffee-klatsch in a corner of that good party
which had not yet risen to kissing.
You were in your mid-twenties and the other four
were in their teens or early twenties — divine ages all —
and I was already four years beyond
that decade when some idiot claimed,
with a drowning man's grasp on a grain of truth,
life begins. Given precocity in the one divine activity
where I never was given it I could have fathered the five of you.
So I looked at the joy and the loving amusement on the
    beautiful young faces
believing there was more love and longing between us than
    trouble and I longed to say 'Yes',
but I had to say: 'You're all young and I'm not'
and that exasperated your generous heart so you said:
'For Christ's sake, you're young!'
so I accepted it not as a drowning man but as one learning
    to swim.

As it turned out the orgy never happened,
we just went on joking and getting drunker and drunker right
    where we were,
and looking at maddening pictures and going a little madder
    than before
but your exasperated generosity
kept me younger for weeks.

The Poet Rides on Horseback through the Night

for Francis Devine

Not flautist but flute-player
not violinist but fiddler
or, if you must,
fiddle-player

> Paddy Rambles through the Park.
> The poet rides on horseback through the night.
> Were you there when they crucified my Lord?

Flute-player not flautist
not Northern Ireland but the Six Counties
not the Maze but Long Kesh
not itinerant but traveller
singing or mending or selling
or drinking too much and breaking heads
just like the rest
and often keeping faith — to music and stories —
the rest would never know
or not have kept.

> Were you there when Amos Barton
> struck up the Flogging Reel? Did you see
> the Fiddler Doyle mount
> the Black Mare of Fanad, to hear
> sea-music? Were you there the night
> Rosario played the Bunch of Grapes
> in the Holly Bush?
> And Trollope in the corner read
> The Eccentricities of Cardinal Pirelli?

Not Europe but the Common Market
though half the world now calls it Europe
as though the vast horror and glory and all the art
of Europe could be so
shrunk down....

    Were you there when Darach Ó Catháin sang
      in a pub in Leeds?
    and the barman said 'We'll have no Pakistani music
      here'
    and Darach's black hair
      glowed blacker still....

Not Great Britain or the U-nited Kingdom
but England: where hungry women
bore bread and blood on a pike,
where Kilvert
watched the fields, where Hudson met
Moses Found, and saw
starling hiding among the sheep, and I saw
near Ripon plover among the sheep.

    Were you there when Militrissa Kirbityevna
      lilted
    Welcome-home-dear-husband-however-drunk-you-be
    for Koba on his keeping, little knowing....

Not America but — some smaller, better name.
Such size may never learn
any small, beautiful name.
But even they might lose their name
when they ride the last big aeroplane,
so not America but Las
Americas.

Were you in the Plover when Paddy Taylor
struck up The Magpie on the Gallows
and then
The Rose Revived?

Paddy Rambles through the Park
we ride on termites through
all but the darkest night.

Affection

Once my name was Clais an Mhictíre
Wolf Hollow
but calling me out of my name they miscalled me
Clashavictory
From hideous murderous clash
                              their victory came
their thoughts ran wild on victory
Clais an Mhictíre — my old name wantoned
earth and animal slain
conquest-gloating

And my name was
                Beig-Éire
Little Ireland
The people who gave me that name
knew affection and fun
                as well as desecration
But the ignorant invaders calling me out of my name
their tongues bloated with conquest
reduced Beig-Éire
to Beggary
       Island
as the whole island — all Éire Mhór —
was beggared, and is beggared in the mind:
the glade-scriptoria desecrated,
latrines paved
with tiles from a synagogue,
the hands of music
                cut off in sport

Burnham Deepdale

Once in a dark porch in Burnham Deepdale
we looked at a very small stained-glass window
at human level, you could touch it:
The Sun, not afraid to come in.
A big, round, golden, beaming face,
filling the whole small space of glass,
blazing away merrily, lighting and warming,
not scorching — mo bhrón géar! —
the blighted clay, the drúchtín crushed. . . .

That big, round, golden, beaming face
more beautiful than Blake,
Palmer's apple-orchard etching,
shone, eight centuries young.
The Armagh apple-orchards too
have bloomed eight centuries beneath
an Iron Crow's claws.

That small, vast sunniness enclosed in dark stone
under the infinite, serene, sequent, billowing
clouds of Norfolk,
the highest skies in Europe —
hot yellow glass sunbursting the tomb —
glowed at human level, arm's reach;
but the Five Grey Sisters cannot be touched,
are out of us, are higher than any benign
friendly Norfolk heavens, they lour, iron-grey,
battleship-bleak, they rule the waves of pity,
they outstare
Barnsley Main Seam.
Eternity's filled their tall, shoulderless, hipless,
narrow straightness, with silencers,

but they make an ugly noise like helicopters
over the green garth of Derry,
over the apple-orchards. . . .

So how can folk whose very breath
is continuity ever understand
us whose breath is broken, whose old gold glass
they've broken, made us break,
make us break still?

The drúchtín trampled under conquering hoofs,
the maiden broken, her May broken,
the searching girl her sweet cheat gone,
her drúchtín lost, the dew undone —
that gentle rain — the springtime and the altars
broken as if for ever,
no glass-painters left even in Blandford —

What might altars matter, cóuld the girl find again
her little white slug in a green garth on a May morning?

Is the continuity merely a papering-over,
an endless combat-jacket?
sang-froid just a strait-jacket?
Does Ermin Street run crooked after all?

But in Burnham Deopdale — spell it right —
the sun was full on,
it glowed like the Book of Kells or butterbrot,
as if no iron crows had ever scratched
the face of summer, it shone full
on the white back of her little drúchtín
before the cavalry came down, on the dead face
of a young girl mar thug sí féin
an samhradh léi go deo.

Clear the Stove in the Morning

for Mícheál MacGarry

Clear the stove in the morning
like clearing the decks for action
last night's goulash now congealed, faintly
distasteful, empty
the teapot, rinse, clear the stove for action.

The water boils, take down the caddy, place
its lid upon an unlit jet, unlid
the teapot, where to put it? place
one lid upon the other, speed
is all, the water's going off the boil —

The teapot-lid entirely hides
the other: it might as well not be there
suddenly it's *not* there
and that reminds the morning potterer
of an early-summer garden
a whole year back:

Door-bell rung twice, no answer, the friend not in,
walk down the short path, between the narrow grasses,
that faint suburban sadness when a door in sunshine
fails to open, then halt: the eye caught suddenly
by something covered, something covering:
on a dandelion, a butterfly!
Now you see it, now you don't!
Human, creep close; quiet; watch:
the red-and-brown creature, wings wide,
as if suspended, motionless, an inch above the grass,

completely hiding the flower — looknohands!
a bit like a boy on a bike — still,
a flutterby not moving?
wait — intruder, leave;
but once outside the railing, glance back:
the butterfly is still there,
held in air,
the yellow still invisible,
that small space between membrane and grass
resembling a mystery — go home and put the kettle on;
   remember.

Flowering Stump

The stump of an apple-tree breaks into flower
against a prison-grey wall.
Trapped in speculation's path, what up to now
was a fine full tree, bearing fruit
forbidden to me but not to children,
was by the builders left
three stumpy arms,
half its old height.
From childhood I could almost box that fox
just by leaning out the window, can anyone see now,
crossing the morning grass that vulpine ghost,
grey as a jail wall? for eight months
I've kept the curtains closed against the building noise next door,
the sight and stench of a dross calf enthroned,
for a month, noise at an end, kept them closed
against the new grey wall
dull matt menacing almost as bad as a prison wall,
prisoning away from me the gentle curve
of Dublin hills I lived with since a boy,
the grey stone mass permits
no near tree, no far hills —
these three pitiful stumps the hackers left
are not a tree — but now!
how can I keep the curtains closed against
these brave white flowers!
Three small blossoms, a few green shoots
on the lowest, nearest stump;
three days later,
the high stump flowers,
next day the third as well is green and white,
it's truly as if the tree is telling me,

telling its mutilators,
telling the prisoned, imprisoning builders,
telling all demolishers and all money:
You haven't killed me yet.
You can't kill me — yet.

Morning after morning, for a brief season,
morning after morning, fox-ghost forgotten,
I open curtains, for big windows thankful,
and watch the green and the white,
the tender green, the vivid white,
waving in front of a prison wall,
breaking the prison,
breaking into and out of that prison,
demolishing it for me for a brief season.

For a brief while we wait, in vain, for fruit,
green lasts longer than white,
who knows what new destruction another year may bring,
who knows what fresh fruit?
Like living things the darker-grey shadows
of coloured leaf and twig
move in the sunny breeze across the pale-grey wall
demolishing, enhancing, building,
re-building hope

Bright Red Berries

Bright red berries, bright-dark-red,
thronged in a small tree's dullish green,
between the women's convenience
and the brand-new Luxury Apts.

The small tree is still there,
it brings forth its berries against
the dull dark-red prison brick,
the grey monoglot piss.

It used to survive behind railings,
on a narrow patch of drab grass and empty cans,
behind it prouder trees and a proud house.

Luxuriant bulldozers ground
the house down, grass out, grew
bijou brick barbarity.
But still the tree stands, by grace of greed.
The gloomy belvedere maws must
have more than convent and garage
to mint-julep at.

Beside the broken footpath, a small tree still brings
colour and fruit forth

Bad Milk

Four-days-half-solid, the milk,
held over the sink, is loath:
it bucks and gouts
under my hand urging,
chugging, the squat bottle:
thick blobs of curdle, thrawn
to block —
        my hand sees again
the stricken mammoth head down,
tongue out, the big dark neck
straining, convulsed; coughing,
slow, painful, out
onto the sand the gouts of blood.

A True Story Ending in False Hope

for Martin Collins

The barman vaulted the counter
landing with a fine clatter
beside our musical table;
he nearly upset the pints
of all the dominical couples.
'We'll have no music here,'
he roared, bursting a blood-vessel.
We weren't, in fact, a steel-band,
or a demolition-squad,
so Justin gestured the tin-whistle
towards the married couples:
'Does anyone mind this
                        music?'
Some said they didn't,
the rest sang dumb,
but one old woman spoke up loudly:
'We like it,' she cried,
'it brightens things up a bit here.'
The barman burst another vessel.
'Out! Out!' he shouted.
'We'll finish our drink,' said the Corkman,
the Corkman who'd *asked* for the music,
and we did,
but we left —
uttering suitable imprecations.

We crossed the unmusical road,
skirting a public jax
that hadn't yet turned into a ghost,

boarded a chopper for heaven,
and played and drank till closing-time,
thinking how musical
Ireland
 will
  be.

Traffic-lights are Dangerous

The cars mount the pavement, break the lights
which don't last long enough: old people just about
make safety, the cars break the lights, raid the footpath
right outside the barracks, a squad-car
zooms out at once to catch the culprit
through night parks of dread
(it does an' my Nobel Prize).

I make it safe home, and climb the stairs
to borrow sugar from an old
old woman, there's an apple-segment
in among the sugar:
                    to keep it dry, she says.

The lout leaps out, from his big shiny car,
and tells the man he's nearly killed:
'You take my number; right?
And I'll get you.'
The rip-off republic cherishes o.k.

I climb the stairs to borrow tea,
there's orange-peel nestling in the caddy,
'I'm all fruit,' she says.

You toucha my car: I breaka your neck,
one sticker grates — and to think that we thought,
in '45, the war was fought
against that kind of bullshit.
Shift your ass, another windscreen screams —
it's a wonder they can see to drive. . . .

I climb the carpet, the leaking roof
has washed one step quite bright,
and hear the old old woman
singing to her windowsill ring-doves
in a high, young girl's voice.

Manifest Destiny

That every county in this developed state
sprout its very own
Ballyporeen: stone-crop, small potato, jackstone.
That's a must, a summit priority.
The tourist bounty, the NATO fall-out,
could solve — dissolve — the Border overnight.

With small-potato-lounges in every single county,
wouldn't the tyrant be proud of us?
He wouldn't even have to murder us.
Next time he calls
let's all
crawl
on naked knees and one hand — the other
tugging green plastic forelocks (there's a thought
for the IDA) — to as near as we can get to the Dáil,
our Dáil,
our, the people's, parliament,
and beg his majesty, this highest king,
via petitions clampt in our gums or green plastic teeth,
signed by all five thousand million
inhabitants of this developed state,
to let us become the fifty-second
state of the union — if any uppity rainbow
dares to show itself higher than this most ardest rí,
why shucks we'll shoot it down,
lower than a snake in a waggon-track,
with missiles the milk-thief lent us —

And speaking of her, we might as well while we're at it
petition for re-admission to the Empire —

no not the commonwealth or common poverty
the old Empire itself, for nothing less
can satisfy
our plastic forelocks.
We thus could be
ruled by three
which is much better
than one-and-a-half.

But for all this glory to come to pass
we must work night and day
might and main
to ensure
that every future incumbent of the White House
can, with cross-channel help,
trace his glorious descent back
to one or other manifest destiny village in the ould sod.
It is of course just possible
that some Chicano, Black, or Jew
might throw a bleeding-heart spanner in the works,
paint the white house black or even rainbow-coloured.
The danger is remote; but should it happen,
after the button's pressed, and we're all born again,
that need not faze us, we can always find,
even for black or jew or nicaragüense,
a touch o' the shamrock, a drop a the oul' crater,
the ever-new volcano — the Limerick pogrom
and the Sack of Baltimore might yield
some helpful hints. . . .

Climbing High

When a man can't say sorry to another
though he knows full well he should
when a man can't apologize to another
though he *knows* he *should*
when he can't spare
two syllables
or perhaps three an' a half
because it might, in court, be considered
an admission of liability
then we have climbed
into a plutocrat heaven
where *only* money talks

It always talked the loudest
even before it was born
but up to
    not so long ago
some other hints got heard
at least they kept a flag flying
and through its tatters you could glimpse
once in a blue slump
humanity
and even that poor young eejit
once called Christ

But now that a man can't
say sorry to another man
though he knows full well he should
and only because of money
because of money only
then we're climbing high
on a gallows without end

The Lost Garden

I spoke to her as one child to another,
as the child I was
              to the child she is,
as the child I remember, who is, remembering,
still here.
And, in part, she understood me.
As I, in part only,
understand.
I spoke to the child she still is,
and also, perhaps, to the woman she'll soon become.
I spoke to the child who plays in the garden I grew up in,
am not, now, allowed to enter;
can still — still —
watch.
Oh I spoke to the sweet-natured girl who can play there
to her heart's content,
for a while yet.
I spoke to the child,
in the mind only.

31 July 1983

Elexía do Caurel

Owl singing in the quiet night
in the shadow of mingled boughs,
you turn these city trees
into an old wood where I always was.
Your song knows nothing of the houses
heaped up all around us,
so I can forget they were built.

You and I weren't made
to live here.
We're both from a long way off
and someday we'll go back there,
where our mystery may be adjusted.

You'll go before I do,
some night when nobody is watching,
in this city of clouds and slow bells.

from the Galician of Uxío Novoneira

Andalusia

At blazing, sweating lunch-time
the Andalusian building-workers erupted into the Catalan
   pub
downing work-dry litres of black dirt-cheap wine
guzzling their own big sandwiches but first of all erupting
six or seven at a time
down the three steps from the narrow street glare
into the officially cool Catalan shade;
some thought them noisy, others vital;
they cast their coins on the counter, making it ring!
looking the Catalan publican straight in the eye
as much as to say, We're as good as you,
and we can prove it
                in your own lousy terms.

The day they got their first helmets —
for capital was beginning to pretend to possess a
   conscience —
they came leaping down into the quiet place
leaping and japing and juggling their helmets in the winey
   air
green helmets and yellow helmets and red
stript to the burning waist and loving the bright colours on
   their heads
and not ashamed of it, and not ashamed.

The Catalan binmen, in their yellow costumes,
balancing wickerwork stench upon their heads,
like Andalusian women balancing the glinting water,
weren't all that staid either,
they made a game of garbage.

A Colour-Photo

for Piero and Ariella

    Melita came from Italy bringing barmbrack from Bewley's
aromatic and warm still when she opened the cake-box
on the round black table,
they were just bringing the first batch up the stairs from the bakery
when she walked into the shop that morning
so she got the first brack of the day
and came straight to me: on the round black
table we'd worked at together so often
the brack in its open box was breathing, warm, knobbly.
    blackish and brown, just crusty enough,
we went to work the better for it

O Ariella
her mother at seventy dancing with you in a summer garden
her dying face alight with love and happiness
her long red gown glowing and swirling to match
the glowing grass and the darker lustre of branches
and your white frock and auburn curls
and laughter one year old!

And us, in the north, in March, looking at such
halcyon, heart-breaking, death-defying pictures,
and eating the warm cake your mother brought me

Will you remember when you grow
dancing with your granny on the grass between the trees
a month before she died, her beautiful dying face
alight with love for you and love for life,
knowing she was dying but happy to be with you, her
    daughter's child,
dancing with you in that last summer,
dancing for all your summers

Notes

page 11: Macdara, a Christian name (and the name of a saint who has an island called after him), means: the son of the oak-tree. The Gaelic sentence means: 'Son, don't be breaking a cat: she'll be broken soon enough.' This may seem harsh — not much better, indeed, than calling the pony Leprechaun — but in fact it was an irresistible echo of the remark 'Ah son, don't be breaking a boat', made (in Irish) to my friend Liam Brady in Connemara, and quoted in an earlier poem of mine.

page 12: The island of Mallorca had been under Catalan rule since 1229. On the 2nd of August, 1391, 'diada de la Mare de Déu dels Àngels' (the Feast of Our Lady of the Angels), over six thousand country-people poured into Palma in revolt against regal — and also episcopal — injustice. The authorities managed to divert their anger onto the Jewish quarter. Three hundred Jews were killed. One result was that the Jews were forbidden to practise their religion, own property, or possess arms. By the end of 1391, there had, naturally enough, been many 'conversions'. The story and the names I found in Baltasar Porcel's book on the Jews of his native Mallorca, 'Los chuetas mallorquines' (Barral, Barcelona, 1971).

page 14: The phrase 'in your enlightened times' refers to the long tyranny of Franco, under which Catalan was forbidden, and only the Castilian forms of first names were officially accepted. Gaietà is Catalan, Cayetano Castilian. Gaietà Ripoll was a Catalan schoolmaster, born about 1778. In 1824 he was teaching in Ruçafa, imparting evangelical ideas. A pious woman denounced him to the Inquisition for not bringing his pupils to Mass or making them kneel at the passing of the Host. Locked up and interrogated for two years, he refused to recant. He shared both his clothes and his food with his fellow-prisoners. On the 29th of June, 1826, in Valencia, he was condemned to be hanged (over the cardboard flames), as 'a dogmatizing heretic and perverter of youth'. The sentence was carried out twenty-four hours later. His last words, 'Crec en Déu', mean, in Catalan, 'I believe in God'. By the time the Editorial Selecta, of Barcelona, published Jordi Ventura's book, 'Els heretges catalans' (The Catalan Heretics) in 1963, there was a certain thaw in the ban on Catalan; but it still took courage to bring out a book on such a theme.

Emma Goldman (1869-1940) went from Russia to the United States of America when she was seventeen. By the turn of the century she was a famous anarchist leader. At the end of the 1914-18 war, during which she had been a pacifist, she was deported back to Russia. Her massive and magnificent autobiography, *Living My Life*, was first published by Knopf in 1931, and reissued by Dover in 1970. In Chapter 52 she vividly describes her meeting in Moscow in 1920 with Maria Spiridonovna, who was by that time even more disillusioned with Lenin than Emma herself was becoming. It's from this account that I got the main matter of this poem, including the cherries and Maria's parting gesture. According to Goldman, Spiridonovna was a member of the Socialist Revolutionary Party, and in 1905, at the age of eighteen, had carried out her party's instructions to kill General Lukhanovsky, Governor of Tambov Province, 'the notorious executioner of the peasants'. She was sentenced to death, but international protest got this commuted to Siberian exile for life. Released in 1917, she — like most of her party — soon broke with the Bolsheviks, 'considering peace with the Kaiser a fatal betrayal of the Revolution'. She was arrested, imprisoned, escaped, re-arrested, re-imprisoned, released because she was ill. When Emma Goldman met her she was, despite her release, on the run. Like the country-people who wrote to her, she 'had taken the meaning and purpose of the soviets literally', and they wouldn't wear the Bolshevik middlemen: the commissars.

Antonio Machado once wrote to Unamuno that he never finished a poem without at once wanting to write another one to contradict it. I feel a bit like that about this poem, though 'contradict' might be putting it too strongly.

page 15: *The Kid on the Mountain* is the name of a slip-jig. 'A tremble of light in the leaves' is the translation of a Castilian phrase from an essay by Unamuno.

page 18: *Amhrán na mBréag:* The Song of Lies. Also known as An t-Amhrán Bréagach: The Lying Song. Songs of this kind used to be quite common in Irish. They were often used as lullabies. Bréagadh, as a verb, means to cajole, coax, or soothe. Whatever about their uses, though, it's clear that these songs allowed the people who made them up to give free rein to their imagination. I just lifted lines I liked from three or four examples in *Clár Amhrán Bhaile na hInse,* by Ríonach Ní Fhlathartaigh (An Clóchomhar, 1976). Mícheál Mharcais is the only author named, and his version was collected by Éamonn Ó Conghaile from Beartla Ó Conghaile, of Cárna in Connemara, in 1952.

page 26: The poem preceding this, in Máire Ní Cheallacháin's edition (*Filíocht Phádraigín Haicéad,* An Clóchomhar, 1962), is called 'From France to Ireland to the same man's foot the time it was broken.' 'The same man', the 'dear one', was Éamann (Buitléar) an Chuirnín.

Haicéad was a Munster Dominican, born somewhere around the beginning of the 17th century, who studied in Louvain and then lived in France for some time before coming home. Not much is known of his life, apart from internal evidence, but he was back in Louvain by 1652, and would seem to have died there two years later. His last extant poem is entitled: 'After hearing that the Irish Dominicans have been forbidden to write poems or songs.' It ends with a curse.

page 27: The Gaelic in lines 8 and 9 means: 'you simpleton! you finished fool!' ('finished' here standing for utter, out-an'-out). Under 'pleidhce', Ó Dónaill simply gives 'simpleton, fool'; but the entry for the same word in Dinneen (whose great work Ó Dónaill himself has rightly described as a thesaurus) begins like this: 'a stump or stake, a flake, a roll, a bundle of rolls of carded wool (about as many as would be put together in a dildurn); a fool...'

page 28: Umberto Saba was born in Trieste in 1883, and died in Gorizia in 1957. His father, whose surname was Poli, was from Venice. He left his wife, Saba's mother, who was Jewish, before Umberto was born. The poet always remembered with love his wet-nurse, Peppa Saba, who came from Slovenia. Saba, in Hebrew, means bread. In 1944 the poet had to leave Rome, where he'd been living, to escape anti-Jewish persecution. He lived in hiding in Florence until the liberation.

page 29: In Pedregalejos, near Málaga, in 1955, 'merendero' meant a bar-counter on the beach, under an awning — whatever the dictionaries may say.

page 33: The title is that of an old Chinese tune. The other titles quoted in the poem are mainly those of Irish tunes and English pubs — though there's also one herb and one painting: Bruegel's *The Magpie on the Gallows* (1568), now in the Hessisches Landesmuseum in Darmstadt. 'According to Van Mander, Bruegel means here that those who speak evil should be condemned to the gallows... in an idyllic landscape stands the gallows with the magpie on it, while to the left peasants are dancing. Van Bastelaer sees in the theme a reference to the situation of the Netherlands, where all that seemed serene was potentially dangerous. Faggin interprets the subject as an allegory of the despotism of Philip II, which could never succeed in depriving the Flemish people of the sun or of the joy of living; and he sees the work as a triumph of light and air.' (Arturo Bovi: *Bruegel*. Thames and Hudson, London, 1971).

Darach Ó Catháin is one of the greatest living Gaelic singers. I was with him when the barman said that.

When Stalin was on the run before the Revolution, he went by the name Koba.

page 37: The phrase 'mo bhrón géar' means: my sharp sorrow (bh = v). In 'drúchtín' the *ch* is guttural, as in loch. Here's part of what Dinneen has to say about it: 'a light dew; a dewdrop; a species of small whitish snail, a slug . . . On May morning girls discovered the colour of the hair of their future husbands from the shade of colouring of the first drúichtín they found . . . Mar d'fheartaibh an drúchtín tsúrthaoi an crannchur sin, / Ní h-aithreach atú tríd shiubhal Laoi Bealltaine', since by the virtues of the white slug you seek that destiny, I do not regret your May morning's walk (H.) . . .' H. is Pádraigín Haicéad, who (unlike Dinneen but like Ó Dónaill now) spells drúchtín without the first *i*.

Iron Crow: Crossmaglen term for helicopter.

Five Grey Sisters: stained-glass windows in Yorkminster.

Barnsley Main Seam: a small model, in a glass case, of men working away at the coal-face, it's tucked unobtrusively into a wall amid the Gothic splendours; and the caption beneath it reads: 'The tribute of the miners of Yorkshire to the Minster.'

Deopdale: 'Deep', in the present spelling, is just a corruption of an old word meaning dale.

The Gaelic in the last two lines means: 'for she took the summer with her for ever.' 'Thugamar féin an samhradh linn' is an old Irish May-day song, usually sung by young girls.

page 53: Uxío Novoneira was born in Parada de Caurel (Lugo) in 1930. His book *Elexías do Caurel* came out in 1966.